Qualified *by* God

DR. FELICIA O. A. DENNIS

Qualified by God

BY: DR. FELICIA O. A. DENNIS

Qualified by God
Copyright © 2022 by Dr. Felicia O. A. Dennis
Published by Grace 4 Purpose, Publishing Co. LLC

All rights reserved solely by the author. No part of this book may be distributed, posted, reproduced, or stored in a database in any form or any means without the prior written permission of the author.

Scripture quotations from The Authorized (King James) Version. Rights in the Authorized Version in the United Kingdom are vested in the Crown. Reproduced by permission of the Crown's patentee, Cambridge University Press

Editing by: Grace 4 Purpose, Publishing Co. LLC
ISBN-979-8-9908003-0-4
Book cover design by Untouchable Designz and Consulting
Printed and bound in the United States of America

TABLE OF CONTENTS

"Trust in the Lord with all thine heart; and lean not unto thine own understanding. In all thy ways acknowledge him, and he shall direct thy paths".

(Proverbs 3:5-6)

DEDICATION

This book is dedicated to God first and then to everyone that ever struggled or was made to feel that they did not qualify according to the rules of man. My desire is that this book will provide information, inspiration, and illumination to those that find themselves reading and applying the principles making an amazing impact. I encourage each reader to jump into the deep while learning how to increase your faith. First, continue seeking God on a daily basis for how to become more like Christ. Second, strive to build meaningful relationships with individuals that will challenge daily growth beyond the church walls into community. Third, never allow anyone to make you feel disqualified causing a spiritual death but keep the fight to be able to enter eternity with God.

Know this one thing, we have a special calling, and it was given to us way before we ever entered into our mothers' wombs. In life there will be some high and low days that each of us have to face that will include mountains, valleys, joy, pain, and peace. There will be times that we feel like throwing in the towel and giving up, but we must stand firm on what it is that we are. When those days come, seek God through reading His Word, prayer, praise, and worship. Plus, always remember the words of Isaiah "No weapon that is formed against thee shall prosper; and every tongue that shall rise against thee in judgment thou shalt condemn. This is the heritage of the servants of the Lord, and their righteousness is of me, saith the Lord". (Isaiah 54:17)

SPECIAL DEDICATION TO MY BELOVED PARENTS

This special dedication is to my beloved late Mother, Catherine W. Dennis-Holmes, and late Father, Furman M. Dennis, Sr., for being the parents God chose for me. Thank you both for always loving me in your own special way and guiding me through this journey of life the best way you knew how. Even though the two of you are no longer here with me on earth you will always live through me by way of your DNA. Queen Mama, please know that I can still hear your voice and love guiding me and you will always be my first best friend and remain in my heart forever. I love you both and miss you dearly.

SPECIAL THANKS

A special thanks to Grace 4 Purpose Publishing Company, of Atlanta, GA for all your diligent efforts, patience, and professionalism in assisting me to complete this book. Your work was EPIC! Won't God do it! Yes, He will!

"No weapon that is formed against thee shall prosper; and every tongue that shall rise against thee in judgment thou shalt condemn. This is the heritage of the servants of the Lord, and their righteousness is of me, saith the Lord".

(Isaiah 54:17)

INTRODUCTION

Is this just another book to read? No! We believe this book is unique because its emphasis is not just on the disqualifying status (girl, boy, woman or man), but on how everyone in their own right is *Qualified by God.* We want to direct the reader's attention toward the characters within the bible that should have been disqualified due to their family history or something they did. Many go through life believing that they will only become a product of their environment, but every man, woman, or child has the abilities to succeed beyond. This book is designed to nudge each reader closer to God, while feeling God's everlasting love.

Beloved, *Qualified by God* is not about finding the uncomplicated way out, but being able to not crack under pressure. It focuses on eight days of godly men and woman found in the Bible that went through their process to be qualified. This book will not only enhance your love relationship with God, but also guide you as a believer, support you in the trials of life, and comfort you in times of weakness. As you read you will see how each individual found themselves making it through the storm to victory. Many of them recklessly abandons themselves to their

Lord and Savior, diligently uses their days of testing, trusts God with unwavering faith, demonstrates loyalty in daily life, and loves God wholeheartedly.

What are you waiting for? Is it for the approval of man, the guest prophet to give you a word, a dove to fly by and give you a sign? What if the approval of man comes, the guest prophet does give you a word, the dove for sure come and gives you a sign? Will it give you the fire that you needed to know that you are qualified? So come and explore *Qualified by God* and learn how The Process of Life Qualifies You Too.

"Many are the afflictions of the righteous: But the LORD delivereth him out of them all".

(Psalm 34:19)

DAY ONE – ABRAHAM

Abraham was chosen by God to do mighty works; however, his lineage did not qualify him for the call, but his relationship with God did. God changed his name from Abram to Abraham for he would be a father of many nations as God made him. Abraham was also known as the first prophet in the Old Testament.

We find that Abraham's lineage should have disqualified him, but it did not because he was chosen by God from among a wicked people that worshiped the moon just to become the father of the nations as we know them to be the nation of Israel. Abraham's descendants from the wicked city of Ur should have disqualified him from being used by God because his people came from a lineage that were given over to idolatry and the worship of the moon god cult, but the Almighty God had a plan for Abraham's life.

Abraham did not allow the carnality of lying lips and a deceitful tongue stop him from responding to God's call nor cause him to reject the covenant he made to God. Never once did Abraham question God when approached, but he came out of his comfort zone and embraced the call by responding to God and relying on the covenant. He was the one that was selected and chosen to redeem the name of his people and to walk away from their beliefs and teachings to become the father of a great multitude.

The most powerful thing about the life and lessons of Abraham is that he found faith in a God that he did not know. This same faith assisted Abraham with embracing fatherhood even at an old age for he and his wife, Sarah. Abraham allowed God to change his name from Abram to Abraham totally trusting God to deliver every promise that He said. The overall blessing is because Abraham found faith, hope and trust right away, this caused him to become qualified for the covenant assignment with God.

Abraham displayed great faith as a leader, was the father of Hebrews and became very fruitful as God promised. He was truly an example of what we would call a righteous man. The most amazing thing about Abraham is he still believed despite impossible odds that were before him, and because of this he had great faith in the promises of God. We know that he was a God-fearing man even before he truly knew who God really was and for this very reason Abraham allowed his obedience to bless him.

Even today Abraham is used as a model and a reminder as a prime example concerning faith when it comes to Christian believers.

We find that Abraham didn't just have faith as a leader, but also had faith as a father concerning the birth of his promised son Isaac. Just as Isaac was promised to Abraham and Sarah in Genesis 18:10 for an everlasting covenant and seed after them, so was Jesus promised to Mary and Joseph in Luke 1:31 (King James Version). Abraham had a major assignment, just as Joseph did, to birth the seed of Isaac that would also assist in saving his people from their sins.

Jesus did the same when he died on the cross for our sins in the New Testament to save us all. Both Abraham and God had the responsibility of offering up their sons to fulfill their covenant. It is especially important that we understand that Abraham's relationship with God is what qualified him. God had grace for Abraham, a man that came from a pagan people, and saved him through faith. Even at the age of ninety-nine years old that Abraham was, he displayed great fervency for the Lord by finding himself in the heat of the day running to meet Him showing accountability as a friend.

True friends fellowship with each other and operate with the spirit of familiarity like Abraham did when it came to the Lord, for he knew the Lord on sight. Many times, as believers today we say that we know the Lord as Abraham did, but we have a challenging time recognizing Him through His Son Jesus Christ, because there has never been a true encounter or relationship with Him in the first place.

Abraham was also identified as God's man for a few distinct reasons and had the opportunity to speak to the Lord very honestly and directly because they were friends. The scripture reminds us in James 2:23, that because "Abraham believed God, and it was credited to him as righteousness...," that he was called God's friend (King James Version). This is another notable example of why Abraham was chosen to become the father of many nations. God didn't look at him as a servant that didn't know what his Lord does, but He called him friend because he knew who God was and what He could do.

The covenant that Abraham had with God qualified him because when God gave him a name change even at the age of ninety-nine, he asked no questions and just received it and went. Even though Abraham had some concerns that were real, he didn't allow their ages or the promised son to stop the mission that he was chosen to complete and fulfill the everlasting covenant. The only way that the everlasting covenant came to pass was because of Abraham's obedience to God from the very beginning and because of this here we are today.

Abraham had an amazing level of companionship, and it showed in his relationship with others and God, like the wellbeing of the three men standing nearby in Genesis 18 (King James Version). He didn't have a problem with being a servant or offering what he and Sarah had to assist in refreshing others nor did he mind going to the Lord on the behalf of others, fighting for them and asking for another chance concerning their wicked behavior in Sodom and Gomorrah before being destroyed. This is why I believe Abraham was chosen by God to do mighty works. Even though his lineage did not qualify him for the call, his relationship with God justifies him to be chosen to give birth to the promise.

"And the scripture was fulfilled which saith, Abraham believed God, and it was imputed unto him for righteousness: and he was called the Friend of God".

(James 2:23)

DAY TWO – ISHMAEL

Well, we can't move on to talk about Isaac the son of Abraham until we pause and talk about Ishmael, who was indeed Abraham's first-born son. Ishmael's name means "God will hear". Ishmael was Abraham's son born out of wedlock to his Egyptian servant Hagar, due to stepping out of the order and will of God because of being impatient not waiting for the promise.

He was raised up in Abraham's and Sarah's house for the beginning of his teenage years, until Sarah's womb came alive, and she conceived her first child and promised by God to bring forth and complete His covenant called Isaac. He became Abraham's sole heir and because Sarah disliked how Ishmael was treating Isaac, this caused Ishmael and his mother Hagar to be pushed out to the desert causing rejection.

Ishmael was also given a promise by God and that promise was that he would indeed raise up a great nation of his own as well. So, both of Abraham's sons were promised nations and it did come to pass, because they both were his seed. (Gen. 17:6) reminds us of that "And I will make thee exceeding fruitful, and I will make nations of thee and kings shall come out of thee."

So, Ishmael was born into royalty even though he was born out of wedlock and would be considered disqualified by man, he was qualified by God.

Let's imagine how Ishmael felt as a young child to be disinherited and dismissed by his own father and his father's wife Sarah due to Isaac coming on the scene. Throughout Ishmael's life God made him faithful and because of his faithfulness, God blessed him. God increased his numbers, and he became the father of twelve rulers, developing another great nation. Ishmael's tribe also included one daughter among the twelve princes that grew into the "Twelve Tribes of Ishmael." Through the life of Ishmael, we learn that God is a God that never wavers. Abraham and Sarah wavered but God kept His promise despite their doubting and going left rather than staying the course like many of us also struggle with throughout our lives.

God showed us so much about Himself through the life of Hagar and Ishmael. He showed them the tenderness of His heart, how faithful His love is, just as it is also towards us. He also showed what Grace and Mercy looks like when mankind counts one out. He then showed us the beauty of justice when one is oppressed but *Qualified by God*. "This is why it's important never to count yourself out just; because it appears that someone else has.

Ishmael went through a season of his life where he was very angry and because of his anger killing became easy to him. God told Abraham that Ishmael would be a wild donkey of a man. One lesson that we can learn from the study of Ishmael is that God genuinely loves the rejected. He promised that He will never leave us nor forsake us. Beloved, we have been *Qualified by God.* Just like He did with Ishmael, He will take care of us the same. When we cry God hears us and bottles up our tears. Why? Because He loves the rejected and we've all been rejected at some point in time.

Even in man's rejection of us, God still fulfills His promises when man won't. We saw through this study that good can come out of whatever difficult situations that we might find ourselves facing. Remember if nothing more, that we are *Qualified by God*, and no demon in hell can deter God's plan for our lives. There is not one person that can say that following God has been easy, and it sure doesn't mean we will be perfect by no means necessary. God requires us to stay the course and remain in His will always.

One thing that we do know for sure is that God is involved in our lives whether we want Him to be or not. He created us, so He also has all rights to qualify each person reading this and cause us to birth nation's just like those in the Bible given this very promise.

"And I will make thee exceeding fruitful, and I will make nations of thee and kings shall come out of thee."

(Gen. 17:6)

DAY THREE – ISAAC

Isaac was a man of great wonder, miracles, blessings, and worship. Although he had weaknesses and wounds, they were a part of what qualified him, like us, to be used by God.

As we continue to examine the character, Isaac, we find that even though Sarah's womb was barren until God released it at an appointed time bringing about the birth of her miracle child and wonder to his father Abraham who was one hundred years old when he was born. To give a little family history pertaining to the bloodlinc. Isaac's parents settled in Canaan, his father Abraham was seventy-five at the time and childless married to his mother Sarah. God made a promise to Abraham even in his old age and told him that he would inherit the land. Not only did he promise him the land, but that it would become a nation.

Somewhere along the journey Abraham and Sarah lost hope and we find that Abraham stepped out of the divine order of God prematurely. They welcomed Hagar into their private chambers to conceive Ishmael for Abraham because Sarah was barren. The good news was that even though Ishmael was in the picture, God anointed Isaac and established an everlasting covenant with him even before he entered his mother's thoughts and womb. Yes, Ishmael was born first, but remember he was not the seed that God promised Abraham. It seems that Abraham became confused, impatient, and not clear about his assignment and that's why he felt it was necessary to lay with Hagar the maidservant of his wife Sarah.

Even in this, God kept His Word. Twenty-five years later after the promise was spoken to Abraham, Isaac was born, just as God promised. The Lord made it clear that He wasn't taking anything away from his brother Ishmael for he was also blessed and would be made a great nation, but Isaac was the chosen miracle and blessing to come within the next year. This was a fitting example that teaches us how we should wait on God, many times we move out of the Will of God thinking that we are doing God a favor by taking control of our current situation of not producing. God simply wants us as believers to wait because God's timing is not our timing, but His timing is right on time.

Abraham, Sarah, and Isaac were indeed Qualified by God, and God made sure to it that no matter what the child of promise still had to be born. Isaac was a native of Canaan and remained there his whole life, even though he did consider leaving, God told him to stay. God also appeared to Isaac just as he appeared to his father Abraham twenty-five years before his birth, Isaac was promised land, descendants, and a blessing to all the nations of the earth. The beauty of this was Isaac remained faithful as his father Abraham did and God's hand remained at work throughout each generation. Through his obedience Isaac became very wealthy and the crops he planted in the land reaped a hundredfold within the same year.

Through our examination we not only find out about the wonder of Isaac's birth, but we also find that Isaac's father, Abraham, made a request that Isaac's wife not be a Canaanite. He made it clear that she would come from his country and his kindred, making her one of Abraham and Isaac's relatives. Abraham's servant traveled around four hundred and thirty miles from Hebron to Nahor where he found Isaac's wife Rebekah. She not only responded with a proclamation that she would go, but also responded to the possibilities of becoming the mother of many millions. During this time, Rebekah had to go through a period of waiting before there was a joining in wedlock, but she wasted no time making up her mind in making the decision to say yes that she would go with the servant to meet her groom. Somewhere along the line Rebekah also had to come to an understanding that she too was *Qualified by God.* This is the same way that we as believers should be when it comes to saying yes to the things of God when He calls us to His Kingdom assignments as His children. Isaac wasn't just a wonder concerning his birth and marriage to Rebekah.

If we remember, even in God asking Isaac's father Abraham to sacrifice him in his youth, Abraham had no problem with doing so because he trusted God just that much. Think about it, the same thing God asked Abraham to do in Genesis He turns right back around and does the same with His son Jesus, who became the sacrifice for all of our sins in the New Testament. Jesus went through a death, burial, and resurrection just for you and me. Even in this Isaac was *Qualified by God* and had to be born to make a pathway for his legacy and lineage that came forth after him. Even after the death of Abraham the Bible tells us in Genesis 25:11, that God blessed his son Isaac and Isaac dwelt by the well Lahai-roi (King James Version).

Here we find that Isaac had many blessings and was blessed by the Lord with flocks, possession of herds, and a great store of servants. The Philistines envied him. So, Isaac finds himself pitching his tent in the valley of Gerar, a place where his father Abraham once had wells of water and now Isaac finds himself digging the old wells back up again and giving them back their name. Isaac was also blessed to build an altar where he could call upon the name of the Lord while his servants dug a well and not long after they gave a report to Isaac that they found water. I can imagine that Isaac's hope had increased from being weighed down with the grief of his father's death and happiness had set in while being over showed by the blessings of God. It's important even as believers that we trust God and continue to fight like Isaac even through our difficult experiences in life and don't allow the bullies in our lives overtake us under pressure.

The amazing thing about this study is that Isaac was a wonder, received his bride, was blessed, and had many wells along with worship. Isaac was truly a worshiper for he interceded for his wife Rebekah because she was barren like Sarah before God opened her womb. Isaac approached God with incense and asked God with insistence and because of that, God heard him and showed up with divine assistance multiplying his seed as God promised. Here we find that as believers, especially in the year of twenty-twenty three, it's especially important to remain at the altar on our faces before God and not move until He hears our request and shows up to assist with our need immediately. Always remember that God has Qualified you, and me even when man tries to disqualify us.

In summary, Isaac was a man of great wonder, miracles, blessings, and worship. However, even though he had weaknesses and wounds, he didn't allow them to define his future. As a matter of fact, all of this was a part of what qualified him, just like us as believers, to be used by God even through our pain. It's one thing to be rejected, but it's another level when the rejection comes from one within our bloodline or that of one closest to us.

Isaac went through a season of rejection from his brother, Ishmael who was known as a wild and warring man with a mean attitude. I'm sure we all know someone like that in our family too. Generational curses are real, and Isaac's son found himself dealing with the same issues that he and Ishmael experienced. Isaac's sons' Jacob and Esau were divided through actions and association; one was defiant and the other deceitful; one was dealing with the father's distance and the other dealing with the mother's disapproval and feeling like she lost her son.

Sadly, they were divided by anger like many people today that find their families divided by passionate and persistent anger that only God can heal. So, as we continue on with our examinations of some of those within the bible that's *Qualified by God*. We will learn more about the sons of Isaac and Rebekah, both Jacob and Esau who were Abraham's grandsons.

"And it came to pass after the death of Abraham, that God blessed his son Isaac; and Isaac dwelt by the Lahai-roi"

(Genesis 25:11)

DAY FOUR - ESAU AND JACOB

Jacob and Esau are known as Abraham's grandsons and Isaac's fraternal twins to Rebekah, first mentioned in the book of Genesis. Examination tells us that Esau was red and hairy when he was born, later becoming a wandering hunter, as his brother Jacob was a shepherd and the second born son. If you are one that has grown up in church, you would most likely know that most preachers focus on Esau losing his birthright to his young twin brother Jacob and how that later leads to their fallout that led to their separation due to Jacob's spirit of deception. Then if you haven't grown up in the church, this is possibly the first time that you have heard this story pertaining to Jacob and Esau. I assure you not to worry you will be brought up to date as you continue to read along receiving more clarity. Understanding how Jacob was still *Qualified by God* even after his display of great deception to his brother Esau.

This deception came about during the time of their father Isaac being aged and nearly blind, not being able to tell the difference between the two. We all have had family members that have gotten to the point of life where they can't tell who is who.

Then there is family. I'm sure we all know that some parents have a favorite child, and it causes jealousy and envy among the others. Well, this is what we find when it comes to both Isaac and Rebekah's love for the two. Isaac had a bit of a taste for wild game, and we know Esau was a wandering hunter, so he loved Esau as his favorite and Rebekah loved Jacob from his conception. Sadly, to say that there was warring going on between the two even within Rebekah's womb and she knew there was a great division going on.

Rebekah clearly didn't understand why, so she found herself making her way to seek God and as she awaited her answer. God spoke unto her allowing her to know that there were truly two nations living within her womb. He went even a little further and allowed Rebekah to know that there were two manners of people, but they will be separated from her bowels. One would be stronger than the other and not only that, but the elder (Esau) will serve the younger (Jacob) when it's all said and done. Why? I'm glad you asked. They both were *Qualified by* God even within their mother's womb.

In the book of Genesis, it is made clear that Esau was born first, and that Jacob came following, holding on to Esau's heel as if he were trying to snatch his brother back up into his mother's womb so that he could be the firstborn. This is why as parents we must be careful of the names that we give our children because the name Jacob means “he grasps the heel”. Not only does it mean that, it’s also a Hebrew idiom for deceptive behavior, so Jacob came out of the womb with tricks up his sleeve and later on known as the trickster.

Later on in Genesis, we find out a little more about the deception once Esau returned to Jacob begging due to being hungry from being out in the wilderness. Instead of Jacob freely offering his twin something to eat out of love for him, we find that Jacob offered to give him a bowl of stew only if Esau sold him his birthright. This meant that Jacob stole his brother Esau’s birthright, yes that's right, the right to success to Isaac’s promises and blessings. The mind-blowing thing is that out of hunger, Esau agreed to the terms that Jacob laid out on the table before him while being vulnerable. Beloveds know that even in our vulnerability that we are still *Qualified by God.*

As we learned earlier, Esau was truly a wild man and because of this Jacob could not remain home after stealing his birthright comfortably. So due to this trickster behavior, Jacob had to pack up and escape from the wrath of his brother. This caused him to have to leave home getting as far away from Esau as possible. It's important that we treat people the way that we want to be treated or we'll find ourselves trying to escape from the choices of life just as Jacob found himself having to from his own flesh and blood. The one thing about God though, He always finds a way to show us His twins, Grace, and Mercy!

After many, many years Jacob had a family of his own and not just that he also became very wealthy. God then showed him grace and Jacob was then able to return home back to his father's Isaac's house located in Palestine. The miracle was that Jacob was finally able to return home and also make peace with his eldest and twin brother Esau. Our God is a God of forgiveness and no matter how long it takes, he's also a restoring God and has restored many families. Even after forgiveness comes, restoration takes place, and we still are held accountable for every decision we've made. That's why there's such a thing called reaping what we have sown whether it is good or it's bad.

Well among Jacob's son's jealousy also arose within the next generation and his youngest son Joseph the one he gave the coat of many colors and was also known as the dreamer who would rule over his siblings. He too was *Qualified by God*. Even after the brothers sold him into slavery to the Egyptian caravan, then tricked their father Jacob by dipping his coat of many colors in blood saying that Joseph was dead. When seeing this we see how generational curses follow good or bad choices from our ancestors, loved ones still here in the physical and ourselves. Jacob was blessed to reap many children and through his children came many descendants. He had two wives Leah and Rachel, two household maids and concubines Bilhah and Zilpah, twelve sons and one daughter. Each of Jacob's sons also had large families that were known as the Tribes or Clans.

Throughout Jacob's life and seeking marriage he served his uncle Laban for a total of twenty years also being tricked to marry Laban younger daughter Leah who suffered from cock eyes first, before having to serve more time for Rachel. Then Jacob found himself serving another six years, during which he amassed a large amount of property, afterward he set out with his wives and children to return back to Palestine to reunite with family. It just happened to be at this time while on the way back that Jacob wrestled with one that some would say was a mysterious stranger, a divine being, or as we would say an angel who changed Jacob's name to Israel meaning (One who strives with God).

God wants to change many of our names just like He changed Jacob to Israel, but we run from the process and are afraid to wrestle all night long for the reward. It's a must because we have *been Qualified by God*, to also birth many nations too. Jacob was blessed to be able to spend the rest of his life living in Egypt after his son Joseph moved him from Canaan! Jacob now Israel was able to bless all of his twelve sons known as the twelve Tribes of Israel before his death.

"And Jacob said, Nay, I pray thee, if now I have found grace in thy sight, then receive my present at my hand: for therefore I have seen thy face, as though I had seen the face of God, and thou wast pleased with me".

(Genesis 33:10)

DAY FIVE - JOSEPH

Joseph was sold by his brethren because of rejection to become the Egyptian Prime Minister giving resources and hope to the Egyptian during the famine. We will find here in the reading why Joseph was indeed *Qualified by God* even after everything that he had to suffer through.

Here in this study, we find that Joseph experiences suffering and the power of his resurrection of becoming the resource of those that are suffering through the Egyptian famine. We find that Joseph lived a good and honorable life when it pertained to God, and he was the only one in scripture that was more like Christ when it came to his person and experience. Once again, God opened up a voided womb and Joseph's mother, Rachel, gave birth to him. With and because of this. Joseph's relationships reveal Jesus. The birth relationship comes into play because Joseph's birth was also symbolic to the birth of Jesus when God also opened a virgin womb whose name was Mary, and she too was *Qualified by God* to birth our savior Jesus Christ.

Then we find that the beloved relationship was between Joseph and his father Jacob, and he was favored by Jacob more than his siblings and Jacob was well pleased with him. I'm sure many of us reading this can relate to their parent child relationship. Because of the father son relationship Joseph's brotherly relationship wasn't the greatest and he found himself being scorned, hated, and rejected. However, life has a way of turning the table and leading Joseph to finding forgiveness pertaining to the treatment displayed to him by his brothers. Later having to be the one that provided the resources of food to them during the great Egyptian famine making him once again *Qualified by God* before his family.

Joseph's rejection reveals Jesus for the same way that his brothers plotted his death and dipped his coat of many colors in blood, so was the coat of Jesus gambled over before Him dying on the cross for our sins. Joseph had a similar trip to Egypt just like Jesus' father took Him and his mother by night and departed there and remained there until Herod passed. The only difference is that Joseph's father Jacob didn't take him there, but his brothers produced a plot and faked his death to his father, selling him into slavery. I'm sure we know of someone or a group of people that has plot against us or someone we love for their own self gain to disqualify us by trying to damage our character, just like Joseph's brothers, but God blocked it and it didn't work.

Once there for a while, Joseph finds himself later being tempted by Potiphar's wife to sin by sleeping with her, but because he rejected her day after day she lied and had him put into prison. Here Joseph finds himself in a place of torture once again in his life after being sold for a servant, being put in jail, and numbered with the transgressors all because of lies of others among him. Even after everything he had gone through, Joseph's ruling reveals Jesus during the time of all the land of Egypt going through a famine. Yes, God qualified him again! Pharaoh tells all the Egyptians to go unto Joseph and whatever he tells you to do, do it. This is when we begin to find that Joseph's resurrection hope reveals Jesus even for his own life when he said that he was not going to remain in an Egyptian grave. We too need to have the same attitude and allow the negativity around us to know that we will not allow it to hold us hostage in a grave of discouragement like Joseph proclaimed and shack ourselves. We are *Qualified by God* too!

Right after the resurrection hope that Joseph found, we see that Joseph's resources reveal Jesus and that the time is coming closer to him having to stand before his brethren and display grace towards them. Beloved, we too can find ourselves having grace for our family members or those that may have done us wrong in times past. God has Joseph in a position now that he has no other choice but to become the resources of God to the Egyptians. There is an open invitation that is given from Pharaoh to Joseph for his brethren to bring his father and their households and to come out of Egypt. The inclusion of God's full resources is that he said I will give you the good of the land of Egypt, and ye shall eat the fat of the land, in other words get your families and come. He didn't only say come, but he told them regard not your stuff; telling them that the good of all the land was theirs. God has qualified us to be that one, yes that one that can lay everything aside and walk in God's will to bring restoration to someone else's life that may be lost and don't know how to be found. Hey, you, yes you! You're *Qualified by God* too, so let's make an impact on purpose.

During the famine that went across all of Egypt they encountered their brother Joseph for he was in the right place at the right time to bless a family that had rejected him and casted him away. He was in a position to assist his brethren that thought he was dead and long gone, for they were living in poverty and had no idea that Joseph was in a place of provision. God will always use the underdog that was cast away by man and lift them up to glorify His name. When Joseph revealed himself to his brethren, he only wanted to know one thing and that was, was his father alive. I can only imagine that they were blown away trying to figure out how in the world did Joseph survive after being put in such danger in his youth.

I'm sure the look on their faces was priceless to have thought that Joseph had been dead all of these years and now they would have to stand before him begging for bread troubled by his presence and their past deeds towards him. He was *Qualified by God* for such a time as this! Joseph shows grace and mercy towards his brothers and never held what they did to him against them offering them the adequate resources just as he did all the Egyptians. I'm not sure of many people that can totally do away with a grudge like Joseph finding himself being about to do out of love.

Here we find the favorable resources of Grace and see the affection of grace when Joseph falls upon his brother Benjamin's neck and wept as they wept together. Then after which, he kissed all of his brethren and wept unto them and talked. Joseph tells his brothers not to grieve nor be angry with themselves concerning them selling him. He allowed them to know that God did send him there ahead of them to preserve life and to save them by a great deliverance. We see great compassion through the kiss and weeping. Sweet communion took place as they talked one to another!

The abundance of giving that Joseph offered was raiment, silver, asses laden with the good things of Egypt, she asses laden with corn, bread, and meat for his father. Joseph finds himself giving them the very thing that they quickly took away from him and assisted in the needs of their appetite showing them grace and mercy. In all of this, we see the regard that Joseph had for them, and the reality is they were still his brethren. This shows just how powerful God is and that He has a way of restoring what mankind feels is broken forever. God doesn't want us as believers walking around in anger, bitterness, or resentment toward anyone for something that was done while they were operating under a demonic force. Joseph had to stand firm so that he protected his character and sent them back with transportation and something tangible to convince his father Jacob in his old age. At the time that Jacob received the message that his son Joseph was alive, it brought about great strength and movement to Jacob. To the point that Jacob wanted to see Joseph before he transitioned, so that he could transition in peace. It's beautiful to know that Joseph moved his father to live with him until it was his time to depart from this world into eternity. If we don't learn anything else from the life of Joseph, know that we can be *Qualified by God* just as Joseph was. He played his role well as a Servant of the Lord living to be a hundred and ten years old.

"But the LORD was with Joseph, and shewed him mercy, and gave him favour in the sight of the keeper of the prison".

(Genesis 39:21)

DAY SIX – MIRIAM

Miriam is the daughter of Amram and Jochebed and the only sister of Aaron and Moses. She is known as the first female prophetess, whose name meant "wished-for child," in the Hebrew origin. She was never married nor conceived children. Miriam, yes, the young 12-year-old who delivered Moses at the Nile River when King Pharaoh of Egypt sent out an order that all Jewish baby boys be killed. This was the way of Pharaoh's so-called population control and that included her newborn brother Moses. She also was the one that led the Israelite women in praise, singing, dancing, worshiping, and playing drums as a sign of celebration and thanksgiving after God delivered them crossing the Red Sea. She would also happen to be the one along with her brother Aaron that challenged the actions and authority of Moses. Miriam is one that will assist us with the understanding of leadership and also how to embrace diverse voices, both female and male as we continue to read and receive the understanding why Miriam was also *Qualified by God.*

This study is written with the hope that we as believers will remain encouraged and continue trusting in God just as

Miriam did. There are times in our lives when we become overwhelmed because so many things are happening around us all at once. However, God wants to make sure that even through everything that we're going through that our response should be, "not my will Lord, but your will be done. "Beloved, He's working in our lives even when we can't see it. See, Miriam was a woman that God used to save a nation through her obedience to His Will.

Imagine watching your mother having to put your baby brother in a makeshift lifeboat and pushing him down the Susquehanna River, trusting that he would be saved from being slaughtered. Well, that's what Miriam had to experience even in her youth, but she didn't allow that to stop her from being who God called her to be. This comes to show us that it doesn't matter the age that we are, God is able to use who He wants when He wants. There may be some youth or young adults reading this study right now and my prayer is that you find hope to press on because you too are Qualified by God just as Miriam and all of the others in the previous chapters.

Isn't it just like God to have Pharaoh's daughter to discover Moses floating down the Nile River and decided to keep him after her father put out a death order on all Jewish newborn boys? Miriam once again watching from a distance and being in the divine will of God, struck up a conversation offering to find a Hebrew woman that would be able to nurse the baby that Pharaoh's daughter thought she had randomly found. Once again this shows another reason Miriam was *Qualified by God.* She made sure that her brother was found safely, then offered her services to find a Hebrew woman and secretly bring her own mother Jochebed. Miriam saved her brother's life and was able to return Moses back to the arms of his birth mother. Beloved who wouldn't serve a God like this that loves us, so much that He would cause even Pharaoh's daughter to have a soft heart.

Throughout time Miriam watched her brother grow up in Pharaoh's house and become one of the greatest leaders in the enemy's territory. When it came for the Exodus of the Israelites from the bondage of Egypt and their journey of forty years in the desert, Miriam once again was on the scene sharing the role of leadership with both of her brothers Moses and Aaron. It's so amazing how God brought this family back together again to lead a nation to the promised land. Miriam walked in great strength and her level of guidance was evident to all mankind who could see. She was *Qualified by God* to lead and because of this as spoken about earlier in this study, Miriam led thousands of the women into dance, praise, singing and the sound of triumphant worship.

Miriam did have her own shortcomings when she wouldn't support her brother Moses and wouldn't sing praises. Just like many of us, Miriam was operating out of her feelings rather than allowing God to lead and direct her spirit. She even became angry with Moses because he decided to marry a Cushite (Ethiopian) woman and felt that he was God's only spokesman. Now doesn't that sound like some of us sisters that feel like no one is good enough for our brothers. Then those that come against you because God is clearly using us as the only spokesman. I've gone through this firsthand and was ganged up on and called everything but a child of God. Even Miriam had some stuff with her that should've disqualified her. Even when she joined her brother Aaron later on in public rebellion against Moses' leadership during that time. Wow! This sounds like someone we know or maybe ourselves at times when we don't agree with leadership and what they have put in place.

Beloved, *we* must be careful and not find ourselves like Miriam after all of the things that she did by being obedient to God's will for her life. When Miriam joined forces with her brother Aaron against Moses, God struck her with leprosy and also rebuked Aaron as well. We must be careful not to put our mouths on the women and men of God. Moses' grace towards his sister because of Aaron's plea caused him to cry out to God asking God to forgive Miriam's sins. Because of this she was healed after seven days of quarantining outside of the camp and was known as the only Israelite to ever be healed of leprosy when it comes to the Old Testament. Miriam also later died, in the wilderness sometime during the Exodus march.

The goal of every study is to show the strengths, weaknesses, and life lessons of each servant of God providing facts to those reading of why they have been *Qualified by God* even after making mistakes. We make mistakes, but we've been *Qualified by God* before the creation of this old world and will remain in His will for our lives.

"Then Miriam the prophet, Aaron's sister, took a timbrel in her hand, and all the women followed her, with timbrels and dancing. Miriam sang to them: "sing to the LORD, for he is highly exalted".

(Exodus 15:20-21)

DAY SEVEN - ELIJAH

Elijah was a Hebrew Prophet and man of God who did not fellowship with the works of darkness but reproved them. Elijah was known as a Prophet and a man of great character whose name meant "The Lord is my God". He was from Gilead which was known as the "hill of witness." He had no problem taking a fearless stand right in the court of Ahab and Jezebel and walked with spiritual boldness to warn them concerning the report of no rain unless he spoke about it. This all came about because of the corruption that was taking place during Ahab's reign and leading a people that worshiped Baal for sixty-two years. The wicked that dwelled there caused a drought that not even the dew in the morning would be able to refresh them during the time of no rain. Sadly, to say, this was a time of no rain that caused food, flocks, and life to be loss. The report that Elijah announced so boldly came with great devastation and pain. I can only imagine Ahab thinking when he received the report. What kind of man could just take a fearless stand and speak such words? One that is *Qualified by God.*

Elijah wasn't just one that had a fearless stand, but he also went through facing the shadows throughout his ministry concerning near death experiences. One of the examples found here in this study is when the woman's son fell ill suddenly. She had no time to go to the prophet Elijah for prayer because things happened so fast, so she found herself blaming Elijah as a result of grief and feeling guilty towards herself. During this time of trial, Elijah trusted God through prayer as he cried out showing fearlessness in the prayer, pleading for restoration of life concerning the boy's dead situation. Elijah as a man had understood that he had no power of his own, but the God that he served had all power in His hands and here once again Elijah was *Qualified by God.* The testimony concerning this trial is that while trusting God in prayer the Lord heard his voice as he stretched himself on the child three times through faith and the soul of the boy reentered his body. By Elijah facing the shadows during this trial, it brought about trust and convinced the woman to believe the words out of the mouth of the prophet.

Elijah was a great man of solitude that learned how to hide from Ahab for God's protection and also so that he could become a man of God. He knew how to pull away and go to his fortress of solitude known as his secret sanctuary as a prophet.

Elijah was not just considered a fearless prophet that took a bold stance, but a prophet that knew how to get in the face of God. It's one thing to hide yourself from someone or something, but it's another thing to understand that your hiding is simply a major part of preparation for your God given assignment. We find that God entered into an agreement with Elijah when it came to the covenant at the Cherith brook not taking away from any of the other covenants, but this covenant came with a sure promise. This promise was casually suggested and clearly stated. In it God commanded the ravens to feed the prophet, Elijah morning and evening and he was to drink out of the brook. During this time of solitude Elijah became established right at the brook all because he trusted God and hid himself for his own perfection while becoming a man of God.

Now that Elijah had become established at the brook, he was now ready to be a fearful servant of God because he knew Him as Jehovah. We as believers have to be so careful that we don't become like Obadiah and compromise with excuses to satisfy the rebukes of our restless conscience. We must stick to the plan like Elijah did and serve God as a fearful servant taking a bold stand before the world around us delivering His message.

That's if we too wish to be *Qualified by God*, like Elijah and so many others.

It is one thing to be a fearful servant, but it's another level to be a fighter that fights with sin at Mount Carmel. Elijah had to stand before people which is somewhat like the people of today that live daily with a lack of knowledge and operating in ignorance. He was amongst the wicked, wayward, and false prophets, but his assignment was to confront the sin, get them to turn their hearts towards God and repent for their sins. Even with Israel's sinful nature, failures and flaws, Elijah still found himself praying in 1 Kings 18:36-37 to the Lord on their behalf asking God to hear him concerning Israel for they have turned their heart back again to God (King James Version). The Lord has a way of showing His power in a way that mankind has no other choice but to bow down and worship Him with praise.

God challenges us as believers in Galatians 6:9 with a major command saying, "And let us not be weary in well doing: for in due season we shall reap, if we faint not (King James Version). However, along the way Prophet Elijah found himself at his breaking point and having failing strength after traveling a day's journey into the wilderness sitting under a juniper tree. Elijah, like many of us, finds himself going to God for others, but can't seemingly find the strength to request a breakthrough on his own behalf. Like Elijah, we find ourselves crying out to God that we might as well die because we feel that we are no better than our fathers that came before us. Just as God was the strength of Elijah's life so is He the strength of each of our lives as well. Many of us are hungry just like Elijah, have gone without food, and find ourselves emotionally drained both physically and spiritually, all while running for our lives and pressing away from wickedness. We find ourselves feeling like all we have done has failed and that evil has prevailed against us thrusting us into a lonely place, but God is still yet with us just as He was with Elijah for his work still was not done.

Elijah found himself without strength at times while being a servant of God, but he still had power with God over his enemy. We find that Ahab had become an enemy of God and Elijah the prophet, but God used Elijah to deliver a Divine message to Ahab in 1 Kings 21:21, causing Ahab to discover his sin (King James Version). God clearly reminds us through this study that we may run but we can't hide from the sin that we have committed and the lives that have been affected. God will use us just like He used Elijah to return back to our enemies and bring a message of deliverance just like he gave Ahab through Elijah that caused him to repent and turn away from his sins and wickedness saving his life. Understand this one thing, it doesn't matter how wicked a person becomes, God's Power and Mercy has a way of making man humble themselves and repent like Ahab before the Lord. This is what qualified Elijah as a Hebrew Prophet and man of God who did not fellowship with the works of darkness but reproved them no matter how lonely the journey was or how high the cost became.

"And let us not be weary in well doing: for in due season we shall reap, if we faint not.

(Galatians 6:9 KJV).

DAY EIGHT-JOHN THE BAPTIST

Most of the time we look at a eulogy as something that praises and summarizes the life and works of a person, but to really understand and describe someone is to summarize their life.

We find from the very beginning that John's name, given to him by the angel Gabriel and his mother, had a strong meaning to it. His name meant grace or mercy of the Lord. He came from the lineage of Elizabeth and Zacharias and truly the hand of the Lord was with him from his birth. John had great promise to the point that when he was born many rejoiced at his birth, for they knew that he would be great in the eyes of God. He also would not drink wine nor strong drink, for he was filled with the Holy Ghost even while in Elizabeth's womb. There was also evidence of greatness that John would be a prophet of the Lord and would have to lie before God concerning his preparation and to prepare his way, so that he could give the message of salvation to those that were living in sin among him. John didn't just have great promise, but he also had amazing progress even while going through his desert experience. The people trusted him to pull them away from their homes and their cities to the wilderness in faith so that they possibly could meet God. As we continue reading, we will understand more why John The Baptist, all the way from the womb, why he was *Qualified by God*, to be a servant of the Lord.

John had progressive behavior for the fact that he wasn't spoken about much after his birth, only that he grew up and became strong in spirit. John was almost unknown, but a few years before Jesus began His ministry John broke his silence with a mighty call to repentance and came out of the desert showing himself to Israel. John's prophetical behavior allowed him to operate in the spirit and power of Elias causing him to have the vitality, the victory and the voice of Elijah very strongly rebuking the spirit of Ahab and Jezebel. His prophetic ministry was so powerful that he had a father's heart and was able to turn fathers' hearts toward their children; those who felt that they were failures had hope again being able to turn their disobedience to the wisdom of the just and followers became ready to be prepared for the Lord. John didn't just have progressive and prophetical behavior, but he was also known for his peculiar behavior of having a ministry like Elijah. His eating, dressing and habits were very much the same as the prophet Elijah. We find for sure that

John was truly set apart and that he was real about his service unto the Lord and accepted that he was indeed qualified.

The prophet of the Lord not only had an anointed beginning and amazing behaviors when it came to doing God's work, but John also had great boldness. John was expected even by the prophets that he would come as a messenger to prepare the way of the Lord to assist in making His path straight as Esaias prophesied. His voice was so expressive, and he had no problem with declaring the Word as a spokesman of God to the unsaved. John was very bold and had no problem with addressing his enemies, the Pharisees and Sadducees that he referred to as 'generation of vipers', that had an offspring of bad fruit that was real poison and needed to be rebuked concerning their fatherhood and their falsehood. The goal was to bring them to repentance, so that they would turn from their wicked ways with the hope that their discernment and deeds would change.

The amazing thing about the study of John The Baptist is that he was a unique and a peculiar person from his beginning to his behavior, the boldness of his voice, and now John's Baptism. Just as Jesus came to save us from our sins, John The Baptist had to come to pave the way for the Lord's coming as Elias declared even before John and Jesus' time. The sermon of John's Baptism was clear as he asked the people to repent and change their thinking, turn from the wicked ways of their past mindset, and get into position for the coming Messiah. Christians and John both had great significance in their baptisms. We find here in the studies that John's Baptism was an expectation, and a mark of repentance and Christian Baptism is an effect and a mark of relationship. John had the honor of being the one that God chose to baptize Jesus, for He had no occasion to repent but was coming to fulfill all righteousness for he too was *Qualified by God*, from his mother Mary's womb. John was able to see Jesus in His threefold office as the Prophet, the Priest, and the King of kings and because of this John fulfilled his assignment for God to prepare the way of the Lord.

John's beholding was very obvious for he was truly on a mission with a message from God to witness and was called out to be set apart knowing who his Master was from his beginning. John's record was even more special and caused people to ask, "who art thou" and identifying him as "that prophet," putting him in the likeness of Moses. Concerning John's bewilderment being like a tower of strength, his strength became a reminder of God's promise to him from his mother's womb. God walked with John The Baptist every step of the way as a preacher, through each success, signs and as a prophet and messenger of the Lord. Just like every human, he went through a time of struggle, questioning who Jesus really was and if there was another that he should be searching for to deliver him. John had to go through a testimony of surety to bring about a sure word of proof, promise and a sure word of promotion being reminded by God that Jesus was increasing just like John said that he would, so please do not be offended by the reports that you hear. John's benediction I believe went something like this: He was a holy man that was honest and remained very humbled throughout his success, his exaltation of the Savior, preaching of the Savior, and his perspective of the Savior could only be given him from Heaven.

"Then cometh Jesus from Galilee to Jordan unto John, to be baptized of him. But John forbad him, saying, I have need to be baptized of thee, and comest thou to me? And Jesus answering said unto him, Suffer it to be so now: for thus it becometh us to fulfil all righteousness. Then he suffered him.

(Matthew 3:13-15)

BONUS READ - MOMENT OF TRANSPARENCY

There are so many of us that had to go through hell and back during this journey we call life before it seemed that God even considered shining a light of hope from heaven in our direction. Let alone believing that we could or would ever be *Qualified by God.* It seemed like life served us lemons most times instead of that good old sweet lemonade that we so long for, but somehow God makes all things well when we least expect Him to. Just think about it. Where would we be if God had not stepped in and showed us His grace and mercy? It's a good thing that you asked yourself! You know that grace and mercy that follows us all of the days of our lives!

The thing is we are much stronger than we give ourselves credit for most of the time. We have to remember that we have been made in God's image and likeness, but also understand that there is a difference between the two. We as mankind have been made in the image of God and when people see us, the God in us should be who they recognize and not someone that can't be identified. We operate in the spirit and likeness of God displaying every quality that He has strategically given to His creation. The beauty of this reading and the thought behind the devotional was to show how God takes his creation and qualifies us. Think about it, he made Adam and Eve from the dust of the earth and the spit of His mouth. Yeah, I hear you, yes, it is a nasty thought! However, it had to happen, so that He could mold and make both of them into what He desired for them to be. Even though they failed the test due to the lack of obedience to God's instruction, He still gave them yet another chance to remain and continue their journey, but they had a price to pay. The price we know as sin. Each of us had to be shaped in iniquity, and in sin did our mothers conceive us.

Well guess what? Even though we all had to come this way and enter the world through our mother's womb. God has never changed His mind. This is why being molded and made is the only way that we can truly become *Qualified by God.* There is no shortcut to jump around that process. We must get that stinking thinking out of our minds immediately, so that God can fulfill His perfect work in and through us.

Who would've thought a child fighting for her life in 1980 within her mother's womb would ever become the woman of God that you see today. The funny thing is doctors didn't even believe and said that I would never live a normal human life due to my mother having seizures daily while carrying me within her womb for nine months. That's why it's important for each of us to know who's report to believe and that report comes from God and God alone. The prayers of the righteous availeth much and because of this I have become *Qualified by God*, to assist with shaking up the world while being radical for God and leading the unsaved into the arms of Jesus.

This short transparent moment is simply to open the hearts of each reader assuring them that they too can become *Qualified by God.* There is a making, molding, and purifying process that must be completed daily by living a holy lifestyle that displays the God in us to the unbeliever, so that they too may want to be saved and become the salt of the earth and the light of the world. May the peace of God be with each of you and continue to #WALKINIT, yes complete VICTORY because the "Process of Life Qualifies You Too RIGHT NOW!

About The Author

Dr. Felicia O. A. Dennis is a native of York City, Pennsylvania and currently serves as a Clergy Member at Fairview Full Gospel Missionary Baptist Church, an Activist locally and internationally, a Councilwoman, has an Associate in Graphic Design, a Doctor of Theology and is very passionate about serving, assisting, supporting, advocating to meeting the needs of the youth and families.

Dr. Dennis is the humble owner/founder of Felicia's Tae Kwon Do Karate Studio, LLC, Thou Art And Natural Products,

Felicia O. A. Dennis Missions that also host (FreshFire Conference/Revival), Call To Action Worldwide of York, PA, Boot On The Ground Movement of York, PA, African-American First Fridays and Bridging The Atlantic Tours. Also, serving as the Black Start Action Network International (BSANI), York, PA Coordinator.

Dr. Dennis works in the York City School District's Safety and Security Department and formerly worked for Military Sealift Command as a merchant mariner, in Gaeta on the USS Mount Whitney Blue Ridge class Amphibious Command Ship (Sixth Fleet) and honed her leadership skills.

As a child welfare alumna and clergy member, Dr. Dennis knows what it means to overcome hardships and the difference a hands-up approach can make in someone's life, so it's important "to put in the work with boots on the ground, one step at a time, together."

Connect with the Author

Website:

www.drfoadmissions.com

Email:

foadm117@gmail.com

Facebook:

www.facebook.com/FeliciaOADMissions

or

www.facebook.com/felicia.dennis

Grace 4 PURPOSE PUBLISHING CO.

Grace4Purposeco.com

Made in the USA
Columbia, SC
31 May 2024

36103529R00041